The Mindful Mind

Conquer Overwhelm, Calm Your Mind, Reduce Stress, Improve Productivity & Create A Life of Abundance

Som Bathla

www.sombathla.com

The Mindful Mind

Your Free Gift Bundle

As a token of my thanks for taking time out to read my book, I would like to offer you a gift bundle:

Claim Your Gift Bundle!

Three AMAZING BOOKS for FREE on:

1. Mind Hacking - in just 21 days!
2. Time Hacking - How to Cheat Time!
3. The Productivity Manifesto

Download Now

You can also download your gift at: http://sombathla.com/freegiftbundle

Want something more?

Okay, Click Below to Get Your **FREE REPORT** covering:

11 Free Smartphone Apps to Reduce Stress & Upgrade Your Mindset

You can also Download at:
http://sombathla.com/stressfree

The Mindful Mind

Contents:

Your Free Gift Bundle 2

Part I: Introduction 5

   Search Inside Yourself...............................5

   A Mindful Room..9

   The Inner Secret of High Performers......12

   Is Mindfulness Different From Meditation?..16

   Whether Mindfulness is For You?...........19

PART II: What is Mindfulness? 24

   Origin and Philosophy.............................27

   Mindfulness Is A Vertical Journey 44

   From Corporate to Government: Mindfulness Is Everywhere Now............46

PART III: The Magic of Mindfulness-Mega Benefits 53

   It Changes the Structure Of Your Brain..55

   Meta-analysis of multiple Brain Studies-Numerous Benefits..................................58

   Mindfulness –the Default Mode Versus Direct Experience....................................60

   Mindfulness to cure your bad habits: 66

The Mindful Mind

Mindful Munching to Lose Your Weight: 71

The Benefits of Mindfulness- Summarized 73

PART IV: Mindfulness –Let's Do It ..79

How Should You Sit? 81

Develop Your One-pointedness Muscle .82

How to do it? 83

Stress & Depression: If You Can't Cope Up Alone 89

Mindfulness made Mobile - On the Go ..94

Final Words 97

Thank You! 99

About the Author 101

More Books by Som Bathla 103

The Mindful Mind

Part I: Introduction

****

"What lies behind us and what lies before us are tiny matters compared to what lies within us." ~ Oliver Wendell Holmes

Search Inside Yourself

Let me start with an old anecdote.

There was one old lady in a village. One evening people saw her searching for something on the street in front of her hut. They gathered together to watch what she was doing. They asked, 'What is the matter? What are you searching for?' And she said, 'I have lost my needle.' The people were nice, and they started helping her look for it.

The Mindful Mind

When nobody could find the needle after quite some time, someone asked the old lady, 'the street is big, and the sun is about to set. Very soon, there will be no light, and a needle is such a small thing — unless you tell us exactly where it has fallen it will be difficult to find.'

Old Lady said, 'Don't ask that. If you want to help me, help, otherwise you may get to own your jobs, but don't bring up that question.'

Everyone was stunned and stopped immediately — they asked. 'What's the deal? Why don't you want to tell us? If you tell us where it is, we'll help you find it.'

She said, 'The needle has fallen inside my house.'

Almost every shouted, 'You definitely must be out of your mind. If the needle has fallen inside the house, why are you searching here?'

'Because the light is here. Inside the house, there is no light,' she said. Somebody said, 'Even if the light is here, how can we find something if it has not been

The Mindful Mind

lost here? You'll have to bring some light inside the house so you can find the needle there.'

The old lady laughed. 'You people are so intelligent about small things. But, when are you going to use your intelligence for your inner life? I have seen you all searching outside. But I know perfectly well from my own experience that the thing which you are searching for is lost within. The happiness and the meaning of life are what you are searching for, you have lost within — and you are searching outside. And you are applying the same logic because your eyes can see easily outside, and your hands can grope easily outside because the light is outside, that's why you are searching outside.

Everyone stood there amazed, and the old lady just disappeared into her house. This old lady was Rabia Basri, a saint and Sufi mystic. One of the most influential Sufi women in Islamic history, Rabia was renowned for her extreme virtue and piety.

The Mindful Mind

The above story seems to aptly summarize the madness that has engulfed modern-day man.

Although some of you might think that it is nothing but merely some spiritual or religious preaching, the fact of the matter is that building the foundation of our life by inner assessment is the key to lead a holistic life including achieving the success in the material world. Yes, the old lady mocked people about finding the needle in the street to give out a deeper spiritual message, but the same principles apply to every area of our lives in the material world. Being aware of what is going on in your mind helps you to look at the things more objectively, and you can make better decisions.

> *"The way we do anything is the way we do everything." – Martha Beck*

The practice of getting into our bodies and observing the thoughts, emotions, and the feeling is what mindfulness all about

The Mindful Mind

(explained in detail later). Thankfully talking about mindfulness doesn't raise adverse reactions, which was the case a few decades ago. The application of mindfulness practices is now gaining stronger grounds in all the parts of life.

A Mindful Room

Now, let's have a glimpse of a room, which will help you to see how mindfulness is making its way in modern day life.

The room is filled with a few people sitting in half-lotus position at the floor. One man is calmly sitting on a chair and he tells the people, sitting around, "Close your eyes. Allow your attention to rest on your breathing: The in-breath, the out-breath, and the spaces in between."

Everybody is sitting calmly now and trying to focus on their breaths inhaling and exhaling with their eyes closed. There's a palpable silence in the room. For few moments, all is still.

The quiet is broken a few minutes later when the man declares the exercise over. People

The Mindful Mind

open their eyes, and look around the makeshift zendo. It was a long, fluorescent-lit presentation room on Google's corporate campus in Silicon Valley. This man was Chade-Meng Tan, Google's meditation guru known as Google's *Jolly Good Fellow* and most of his pupils were Google employees. And this meditation class is part of an internal course called *"Search Inside Yourself"*, designed to teach people to manage their emotions, ideally making them better workers in the process.

I was intrigued to note the above in one article[i]. It was further reported that more than a thousand Googlers had been through *Search Inside Yourself* training. Another few hundred or so were on the waiting list to take classes like Neural Self-Hacking and Managing Your Energy in the meantime.

Moreover, that Google also invited[ii] the Zen monk, Thich Nhat Hanh, to its campus in

---

[i] https://www.wired.com/2013/06/meditation-mindfulness-silicon-valley/

[ii] https://www.youtube.com/watch?feature=player_embedded&v=7Pd5Ndg00JA

The Mindful Mind

2011 to conduct a practice-based workshop, in addition to an inspirational dharma talk. He was invited to the Google's campus as part of Google's Optimize Your Life initiative, which seeks to encourage health, happiness, and balance among employees and recognizes that mindful, meditative practices are critical to mental health.

Not only Google, but the article also reports that Twitter and Facebook have made contemplative practices key features of their new enterprises, holding regular in-office meditation sessions and arranging for work routines that maximize mindfulness.

At first glance, it all appears somewhat weird. Someone might think how come technology giant and a modern big data company is putting their employees to spend time on things like mindfulness practices to make their employees more productive.

One would be curious to know what exactly is ticking these corporate giants to arrange these meditation sessions in their organization? What's the deal here?

The Mindful Mind

So, stay tuned. The later sections of this book will explain why everyone is talking about mindfulness today. There is a science behind that. But for now, let's also have a look at inner secrets of some ultra-successful and high performers of the world.

The Inner Secret of High Performers

We all know Steve Jobs is famous for his great ability to create innovative and groundbreaking products. But not everyone knows that Steve Jobs was a pioneer in the use of Zen mindfulness meditation to reduce his stress, gain more clarity, and enhance his creativity.

Jobs was quite specific about how he went about practicing this "discipline" (as he called it). Biographer Walter Isaacson quotes Jobs as saying[iii]:

> "If you just sit and observe, you will see how restless your mind is. If you try to calm it, it only makes it worse,

---

[iii] https://www.inc.com/geoffrey-james/how-steve-jobs-trained-his-own-brain.html

The Mindful Mind

but over time it does calm, and when it does, there's room to hear more subtle things--that's when your intuition starts to blossom and you start to see things more clearly and be in the present more. Your mind just slows down, and you see a tremendous expanse in the moment. You see so much more than you could see before."

What Jobs described above is nothing but a 'mindfulness,' practice that's taught in Zen Buddhism and its Chinese antecedent, Taoism. When Jobs spoke to Isaacson not long before he died, he had been practicing meditation for many years.

You and I can see the power of sitting calmly and observing our minds. When Sir Isaac Newton sat calmly under an apple tree in a state of deep consciousness, he invented the master laws of physics, i.e., the law of gravitation, by the drop of an 'apple'. Later, with the power of his intuition and deeper connection seemingly through his mindfulness, Jobs had been able to create an innovative brand called 'Apple', to entirely

The Mindful Mind

change the way people experience the technology.

There are many other high achievers in different fields of life, who use mindfulness or any other kind of mindfulness practice as a technique to sharpen their mental abilities and seek clarity of purpose in life.

Tim Ferriss, bestselling author of *The Tools of Titans*., also hosts a widely popular podcast show called *"The Tim Ferris Show"* He has already interviewed more than two hundred people from diverse backgrounds including business tycoons, top sports athletes, best creative minds around the world, like Arnold Schwarzenegger, Jamie Foxx, Edward Norton, Tony Robbins, Maria Sharapova, Peter Thiel, Amanda Palmer, Malcolm Gladwell and many more. Tim categorically states that one of the most common rituals or daily practices followed by more than 80% of these interviewees is that they have adopted some form of meditation or a mindfulness practice in their daily routine – a consistent pattern of this secluded practice of being with their own self.

The Mindful Mind

Tim writes about how meditation has helped him[iv], "It (meditation) is a "meta-skill" that improves everything else. You're starting your day by practicing focus when it doesn't matter (sitting on a couch for 10 minutes) so that you can focus better later when it does matter (negotiation, conversation with a loved one, max deadlift, mind-melding with a Vulcan, etc.)." He further writes. "Through 20 minutes of consistent meditation, I can become the commander, looking out at the battlefield from a hilltop. I'm able to look at a map of the territory and make high-level decisions."

The below quote attributed to Abraham Lincoln aptly applies here:

> ***"Give me six hours to chop down a tree and I'll spend the first four sharpening the axe."***

[iv] http://observer.com/2016/12/the-one-routine-yes-one-common-to-billionaires-icons-and-world-class-performers/

The Mindful Mind

A mindfulness practice applied consistently and on daily basis definitely does the job of sharpening of the axe, i.e., by improving mental clarity to focus better and thus perform better during the day.

Is Mindfulness Different From Meditation?

I know this question might arise in the minds of a few people. But why ask this question in the first place? It is because there are some myths about meditation. Most people think meditation is something, which they should be doing during the latter years of life after fulfilling their family responsibilities like their children finishing education, their settling into the jobs, etc. In some countries like my own, India – people think that once their children are married and they have helped raising their grandchildren, they will be free from their responsibilities in life.

Somehow, it is a belief among the majority of the population that meditation is something, which is either for people who are escaping from their responsibilities or

The Mindful Mind

who are abandoning the hard realities of the material world. For some people, it is a residuary activity that should be done when you get older and physically not capable to move around much and then you can simply sit and meditate.

If by any chance, you have that kind of mindset, then starting any form of meditation would seem like going against your established belief system.

This belief system about meditation is not entirely unfounded, because most people who got to the heights of the fame doing meditation are the ones who had left the material world and escaped to jungles or Himalayas. Gautam Buddha left his wife and young son in the darkness of night in his exploration towards enlightenment.

You are a practical human being and understand the realities of modern day living. Therefore, rightly, you cannot fathom the mere thought of leaving your family and escaping to mountains to sit under a banyan tree praying to pray for enlightenment.

The Mindful Mind

Obviously, it seems too impractical and escapist, right?

But I believe by now that you are already getting convinced to some extent about the effectiveness of mindfulness, and are thinking that there must be something otherwise why would top corporate and many high achievers of the world would do it? So let's try to first understand what meditation, is and clear some myth around it.

"Meditation as a practice where an individual operates or trains the mind or induces a mode of consciousness, to allow the mind to engage in peaceful thoughts" – defines Wikipedia.

The simple interpretation is to be more conscious and aware about what's going on in your head, the purpose of that is to disengage you from your thoughts. There is no such prerequisite to physically abandon your family or leave your abode or dodge your responsibilities. You can sit relaxed in the comfort of your home, discharging your

The Mindful Mind

obligations and still reaping the benefits of meditation.

But why I was explaining about meditation in such detail? This is because I want you to revisit your beliefs about mediation and moreover because mindfulness is nothing but a form of meditation. As each meditation practice has different principles or process to follow, so is the mindfulness, which is one of the form of meditation. We will cover the ways in which you can practice mindfulness in the later sections of this book.

Whether Mindfulness is For You?

The simple answer is a big yes. Rather it is quintessential for every human being. Every mind needs to be mindful.

It is our general day-to-day experience that we never seem to be in the present moment. We are either reminiscing our past or worrying about your future and therefore don't enjoy the present moment at all. Worry and stress steals the energy and momentum out of the present moment, which results in lower productivity and average results.

The Mindful Mind

The significance of mindfulness is even more in the modern day world. There are so many distractions thanks to heavy intrusion by technology in our lives. Every moment, our attention is at the mercy of the next beep or notification on our smartphones, so focusing on our key priority of life generally takes a back seat.

Alan Watts, British philosopher, writer, and speaker has rightly put across the mental state of affairs of modern man:

> "We are living in a culture entirely hypnotized by the illusion of time, in which the so-called present moment is felt as nothing but an infinitesimal hairline between an all-powerfully causative past and an absorbingly important future. We have no present. Our consciousness is almost completely preoccupied with memory and expectation. We do not realize that there never was, is, nor will be any other experience than present experience. We are therefore out of touch with reality. We confuse the world as talked about, described, and

The Mindful Mind

measured with the world which actually is. We are sick with a fascination for the useful tools of names and numbers, of symbols, signs, conceptions and ideas".

You'll have noted that big corporations like Google, Facebook, and others are spending funds, and investing the time of their employees on mindfulness practices. While, no doubt these companies care about the welfare of their employees, but major benefits come out in the form of focused attention, better productivity and innovate ideas through these employees with clearer and calmer minds.

Therefore, you must understand that if for-profit organizations are spending money to get their people in the state of mindfulness, it is definitely worth experimenting in your own life to advance your career. Moreover, once you have gone through the magical effects of mindfulness on your brain, mind, and body, substantiated by the scientific research in the later sections of this book, you will crave meditation in your daily

The Mindful Mind

routine, like your daily bath; as meditation is the shower for our minds.

What should you expect from this book?

While exploring about mindfulness, its techniques, its benefits, I realized that the relevant information is so scattered that a common reader will simply struggle to get hold of the crux of the information. Since I have been practicing meditation in various forms or techniques from last few years, sometime deeply engrossed (for days attending meditation camps) and sometime bit irregular, I was intrigued to research deeper into this subject and present the necessary material in the form of a concise book. I don't claim to be an expert or Guru, rather I am on this journey towards exploring and understanding this better..

Here is what you will discover in this book:

- You will briefly learn about the genesis of mindfulness in the eastern and western worlds. You will see the different approaches to mindfulness

The Mindful Mind

and the objective behind that – few approaches are towards spirituality and others will be directly towards gaining benefits while functioning in the outside world.

- You will see how the mindfulness practice is spreading further and deeper in all facets of the modern world.

- The book will explain based on the neuroscience based research how mindfulness literally change different parts of your brain and improves your overall well-being.

- The book will explain to you techniques to do your mindfulness practice and if you feel that you are alone and need some help, you will find information about some widely prevalent therapies.

Now let's get started.

The Mindful Mind

PART II: What is Mindfulness?

****

"If while washing the dishes, we think only of the cup of tea that awaits us, thus hurrying to get the dishes out of the way as if they were a nuisance, then we are not 'washing the dishes to wash the dishes.' What's more, we are not alive during the time we are washing the dishes. In fact, we are completely incapable of realizing the miracle of life while standing at the sink. If we can't wash the dishes, the chances are we won't be able to drink our tea either. While drinking the cup of tea, we will only be thinking of other things, barely aware of the cup in our hands. Thus we are sucked away into the future—and we are incapable of actually living a minute of life."

–Thich Nhat Hanh from The Miracles of Mindfulness

The Mindful Mind

In plain and simple words, mindfulness means just being mindful of what is happening within you, i.e., the thoughts going on in your head, the emotions you are feeling, the sensation or vibrations you are feeling in different parts of your body. It is such a simple process, which every human being can observe in their own bodies.

But it has become our tendency to know what is happening in the world around us; and thanks to the technology, you don't have to make any effort to find out – it beeps upon you to garner your attention at every waking hour. We don't switch off our smartphones ever; nor do we wish to miss any single notification or alert on our phones, because we want to consistently be aware of what's happening around us. If all this outer awareness is creating clutter inside your inner world and you can't observe or feel your own thoughts, emotions or feelings, that is the state of mindlessness, as Ellen Langer, a leading research scientist at Harvard states (much more on that later).

Let's look at few definitions of the term mindfulness:

The Mindful Mind

The Merriam-Webster Dictionary[v] defines the term mindfulness as

"the practice of maintaining a nonjudgmental state of heightened or complete awareness of one's thoughts, emotions, or experiences on a moment-to-moment basis."

Wikipedia[vi] says:

"Mindfulness is the psychological process of bringing one's attention to experiences occurring in the present moment, which can be developed through the practice of meditation and other training."

Thich Nhat Hanh, the Zen master states, "..... I define mindfulness as the practice of being fully present and alive, body and mind united. Mindfulness is the energy that helps us to know what is going on in the present moment."

Jon Kabat-Zinn, creator of the Stress Reduction Clinic and the Center for

---

[v] https://www.merriam-webster.com/dictionary/mindfulness
[vi] https://en.wikipedia.org/wiki/Mindfulness

The Mindful Mind

Mindfulness in Medicine, Health Care, and Society at the University of Massachusetts Medical School states: "Mindfulness is awareness that arises through paying attention, on purpose, in the present moment, non-judgementally,"

Origin and Philosophy

As you might be noticing already that mindfulness has caught the attention of the masses in last few decades and has become part of mainstream thanks to scientifically proven benefits. But the concept of mindfulness is centuries old, though it was limited to only a smaller segment of the population, and more particularly was followed from religious and spiritual purposes.

Let's have a quick look at the past to understand the genesis and the different philosophies around mindfulness.

Mindfulness practice has its roots back to the early teachings of Buddha. The connection between mindfulness and Buddhism is established in the ancient text known as the *Satipatthana Sutta*; translated into English as *The Discourse on the Establishment of Mindfulness* (the word *sati* means *mindfulness*). Therein, the

The Mindful Mind

Buddha lays out the set of mindfulness instructions, guiding the practitioner to place careful attention on four different aspects – or foundations – of experience:

1. Mindfulness of The body (e.g., the breath)
2. Mindfulness of Sensations or feelings
3. Mindfulness of The mind/consciousness
4. Mindfulness of Mental contents

The Buddha's first foundation of mindfulness is the body (which includes the breath), and it is no coincidence that many modern mindfulness practices begin by focusing on one or both of these aspects.

For Buddhists, mindfulness meditation and vipassana are pretty much on the same lines. However, the medical community call it "mindfulness meditation". They are the same to the extent that both are practices of observation of rise and fall. But while a Buddhist would recognize the insight developed in a meditator, the non-Buddhist would likely describe a therapeutic effect, e.g. improved skills and maturity in working with the anger within.

The Mindful Mind

Mindfulness in Medicine, Health Care, and Society at the University of Massachusetts Medical School states: "Mindfulness is awareness that arises through paying attention, on purpose, in the present moment, non-judgementally,"

Origin and Philosophy

As you might be noticing already that mindfulness has caught the attention of the masses in last few decades and has become part of mainstream thanks to scientifically proven benefits. But the concept of mindfulness is centuries old, though it was limited to only a smaller segment of the population, and more particularly was followed from religious and spiritual purposes.

Let's have a quick look at the past to understand the genesis and the different philosophies around mindfulness.

Mindfulness practice has its roots back to the early teachings of Buddha. The connection between mindfulness and Buddhism is established in the ancient text known as the *Satipatthana Sutta*; translated into English as *The Discourse on the Establishment of Mindfulness* (the word *sati* means *mindfulness*). Therein, the

The Mindful Mind

Buddha lays out the set of mindfulness instructions, guiding the practitioner to place careful attention on four different aspects – or foundations – of experience:

1. Mindfulness of The body (e.g., the breath)
2. Mindfulness of Sensations or feelings
3. Mindfulness of The mind/consciousness
4. Mindfulness of Mental contents

The Buddha's first foundation of mindfulness is the body (which includes the breath), and it is no coincidence that many modern mindfulness practices begin by focusing on one or both of these aspects.

For Buddhists, mindfulness meditation and vipassana are pretty much on the same lines. However, the medical community call it "mindfulness meditation". They are the same to the extent that both are practices of observation of rise and fall. But while a Buddhist would recognize the insight developed in a meditator, the non-Buddhist would likely describe a therapeutic effect, e.g. improved skills and maturity in working with the anger within.

The Mindful Mind

It is important to note that modern mindfulness practices are often taught secularly – that is, with little or no mention of their Buddhist connections. Mindfulness practice is often described as a form of mental training as a result, and this can be a helpful and accurate way to understand it.

Mindfulness- Meditation Perspective

Mindfulness, as it entered into the mainstream of western world, was primarily from a therapeutic purpose. It was Jon Kabat-Zinn, who in 1979 sparked the application of mindfulness ideas and practices in medicine. He started Mindfulness Based Stress Reduction (MBSR) program for treating the chronically ill people. These Mindfulness practices were inspired mainly by teachings from the Eastern World, particularly from Buddhist traditions. But the way to explain is entirely secular way.

In his book, *Wherever You Go, There You Are,* Jon Kabat-Zinn describes his viewpoint about mindfulness as below:

> "When we speak of meditation, it is important for you to know that this is

The Mindful Mind

not some weird cryptic activity, as our popular culture might have it. It does not involve becoming some kind of zombie, vegetable, self-absorbed narcissist, navel gazer, "space cadet," cultist, devotee, mystic, or Eastern philosopher. Meditation is simply about being yourself and knowing something about who that is. It is about coming to realize that you are on a path whether you like it or not, namely, the path that is your life. Meditation may help us see that this path we call our life has direction; that it is always unfolding, moment by moment; and that what happens now, in this moment, influences what happens next."

What is the main goal of meditation?

If you pay attention to what's happening within your body, you will notice there is a current of thoughts and emotions flowing through your mind every moment of your life. You can compare the current of thoughts and feelings to a river that mellows

The Mindful Mind

sometimes, but that's overflowing and raging at a different time.

One of the key goals of meditation is to help us learn how to step out of that current and observe it from the shore. As we practice stepping out of the current, whilst observing and do it consistently, we strengthen our mind muscle. It helps to have a much greater chance of gaining control of any emotion, it could be impatience, anger, or shame that threatens to sweep us away.

> *"Meditation is the process by which we go about deepening our attention and awareness, refining them, and putting them to greater practical use in our lives."* ~ *Jon Kabat-Zinn*

You Need A Deeper Why

Jan Kabat-Zinn starts with a very pertinent question before your start your mindfulness

The Mindful Mind

practice. He strongly advocates to first clarify the sole purpose or "why" before you develop any kind of meditation practice. In his words:

> "It is virtually impossible, and senseless anyway, to commit yourself to a daily meditation practice without some view of why you are doing it, what its value might be in your life, a sense of why this might be your way and not just another tilting at imaginary windmills." ~ Jon Kabat-Zinn

The key tenet for effective meditation practice is to have anchor for your attention.

Mindfulness needs an Anchor

Imagine a boat getting tossed around by the ocean's waves. To keep the boat in one place, the captain throws down an anchor. The same thing applies to our minds. If we want to keep our minds in one place, we've got to establish an anchor. And the breath is one of the best ones out there.

Another metaphor from ancient Pali texts explains by comparing meditation to the

The Mindful Mind

process of taming a wild elephant. The procedure in those days was to tie a newly captured animal to a post with a good strong rope. When you do this, the elephant is not happy. He screams and pulls against the rope for days. After a while he realizes he can't get away, and he settles down.

At this point you can begin to feed him and to handle him with some measure of safety. Eventually you can dispense with the rope and post altogether, and train your elephant for various tasks. Now you have got a tamed elephant that can be put to useful work.

In this analogy the wild elephant is your wildly active mind, the rope is mindfulness, and the post is our object of meditation or anchor, i.e., our breathing. The tamed elephant who emerges from this process is a well-trained, concentrated mind that can then be used for the exceedingly tough job of piercing the layers of illusion that obscure reality. Meditation tames the mind.

A useful object of meditation should be one that promotes mindfulness. It should be portable, easily available, and cheap. It

The Mindful Mind

should also be something that will not encourage emotionssuch as greed, anger, and delusion.

Breathing satisfies all these criteria and more. It is common to every human being. We all carry it with us wherever we go. It is always there, constantly available, never ceasing from birth till death, and it costs nothing. Therefore, mindfulness practice through focusing on breath can be done anytime and anywhere.

Mindfulness Makes You Observe like Witness

Besides Jon Kabat-Zinn, who focussed on the meditation practices to get the benefits in the modern day practical and stressful world, Michael Singer, who is the author of *The Untethered Soul*, and a spiritual teacher has shared a great piece of wisdom to explain the mindfulness in a deeply convincing way.

Singer explains that there is a voice or an internal dialogue always going on in your head every moment of your life. As Singer

The Mindful Mind

says: "There is nothing more important to true growth than realizing that you are not the voice of the mind—you are the one who hears it. If you don't understand this, you will try to figure out which of the many things the voice says is really you. People go through so many changes in the name of "trying to find myself." They want to discover which of these voices, which of these aspects of their personality, is who they really are. The answer is simple: none of them."

Singer explains further: "Once you clearly see the disturbed part, then ask, "Who is it that sees this? Who notices this inner disturbance?" Asking this is the solution to your every problem. The very fact that you can see the disturbance means that you are not it. The process of seeing something requires a subject-object relationship. The subject is called "The Witness" because it is the one who sees what's happening. The object is what you are seeing, in this case the inner disturbance. This act of maintaining objective awareness of the inner problem is always better than losing yourself in the

The Mindful Mind

inner situation. To obtain true inner freedom, you must be able to objectively watch your problems instead of being lost in them."

We can easily see the pattern in the above explanation of Kabat-Zinn and Singer. The common pattern is that it is someone or something separate or a distinct (from our breath) that has to watch. If you hear that you have to concentrate at your breath, then it clearly means that you are not breath, there is someone else, who can observe breath. Similarly, if there are thoughts going on in our mind and with practice, we can watch those thoughts, it simply means that there is someone there, who can witness everything, e.g. our body, our breath, and our thinking every moment.

And that is the objective of meditation i.e. to train your mind so well that it can easily disengage itself from the thoughts. The real benefit arrives when your silent mind can hear the cues from the universe to take the next step towards life.

The Mindful Mind

Mindfulness – without Meditation – A Different Approach

Ellen Langer is one of the world's leading research scientists, the first tenured female professor in Harvard's Psychology Department, and creator of what she calls the psychology of possibility—challenging the limits of what we perceive to be impossible.

Ellen focuses on a Western orientation to mindfulness rather than the popular Eastern. As she says, "Meditation is a tool to achieve post-meditative mindfulness. Regardless of how we get there, either through meditation or <u>more directly by paying attention to novelty and questioning assumptions,</u> <u>to be mindful is to be in the present, noticing all the wonders that we didn't realize were right in front of us."</u>

Ellen gave the definition of mindfulness not from an eastern meditative practices perspective; rather she has taken a very practical approach of being mindful by being more aware of your mind and the things around. She explains that people are

The Mindful Mind

working mindlessly relying on the false assumption about them or around the world. In her own words, "Mindlessness is pervasive. In fact I believe virtually all of our problems—personal, interpersonal, professional, and societal—either directly or indirectly stem from mindlessness."

Mindfulness is challenging false limits

As per Langer, mindfulness is challenging and not accepting the false limits assumed by individuals about their abilities. Just to take an example, it was once assumed that humans could not run the mile in fewer than five minutes. Rather, it was said to be 'humanly impossible' to run the mile in less than four minutes. However, Roger Bannister broke that limit in 1952. You will notice that each time a record is broken, the limit is extended. But the irony is that still the notion of limits persists.

Langer tells another example of false limits in her book. She asked her students about what is the greatest distance it is humanly possible to run in one spurt. Now since most of students were aware about the marathon,

The Mindful Mind

so that started with the number with twenty-six miles as the greatest distance humanly possible in one spurt. Some said it could be thirty-two miles. But the reality is The Tarahumara, who are native American people of northwestern Mexico can run up to a whopping two hundred miles. So Langer says, *"If we are mindful, we don't assume limits from past experience have to determine present experience."*

There is one more example to challenge the false limit assumption of one man named Goran Kropp. Kropp rode his bike from Sweden to the Himalayas, summits Everest without a guide or extra oxygen, then rides his bike back to Sweden. Isn't that amazing?

Langer's concept of mindfulness is looking it from the perspective of a psychology of possibility. All limits are created by human beings and most of the times these limits are false and self-sabotaging.

If you are mindlessly accepting the limits on the human potential, then you are not mindful. Mindful requires open mind that

The Mindful Mind

questions assumptions and craves for novelty.

> *"Our life is what our thoughts make it."* ~ *Marcus Aurelius*

Another way of being mindful, as explained by Langer is about asking empowering questions. She states that instead of asking, *"Can I do it?"*; one should ask, *"How do I do it?"*

Anybody can sense the difference between the both questions. While the former question is questioning or doubting about the ability or competence, the latter approach is from the position of openness – as one is trying to explore how something can be done. The importance of asking empowering questions cannot be undermined. As Tony Robbins has also rightly quoted:

> *Quality questions create a quality life. Successful people ask better questions, and*

The Mindful Mind

as a result, they get better answers– Tony Robbins

Another important point to draw home is when we mindfully embrace the process orientation, we remember this guiding principle: *"there are no failures, only ineffective solutions."*

To boost mindfulness, Langer suggests provide some strategies like below:

a. Imagine that people can see your thoughts. Think about it. If you practiced this habit, you'd pay far more attention to your mind, especially in conversations and meetings. This heightened self-awareness would improve your ability to accept new ideas and understand different points of view. It would be easier for you to collaborate with others and find innovative solutions for the challenges in your business.

b. She also suggests the simple trick of noticing five new things about the

The Mindful Mind

people with whom you habitually interact, or the spaces that you occupy.

Mindfulness addresses Depression

Langer also explains how mindfulness can help in tackling depression. The main concern with people who suffer from depression is that they think that they remain depressed every time. But the reality is that there are at least some moments during the day when they feel good. So the knowing that there is a variability in the emotions is very reassuring.

A key part of Langer's work on mindfulness is bringing attention to variability. We're *mindful* when we see the variability in our lives. We're *mindless* when we don't. By bringing mindfulness to our experiences of depression, we can do more of the things that are associated with feeling good and less of the things that make us feel bad.

The Dalai Lama shares this wisdom in these words: "One begins identifying those factors which lead to happiness and those factors

The Mindful Mind

which lead to suffering. Having done this, one then sets about gradually eliminating those factors which lead to suffering and cultivating those which lead to happiness. That is the way."

In the words of Langer, *"No matter what you are doing you're doing it mindfully or mindlessly. There is no other way."*

She states that the magic lies in being aware of the ways we mindlessly react to social and cultural cues. We need to challenge the idea that the limitations we assume are real and so remember that they do not exist at all. With only subtle shifts in our thinking, our language, and in our expectations, we can begin to change the ingrained behaviors that sap creativity, health, optimism, and vitality from our lives. Improved vision, a younger appearance, weight loss, increased longevity, and increased creativity are just a few of the many experimental results that are a consequence of these subtle changes.

The Mindful Mind

Mindfulness Is A Vertical Journey

We can clearly see that while our world is getting more technologically connected and progressing at a rapid pace, a lot of people are feeling mentally disconnected from themselves and from others. This all is due to mindless running behind every other shiny object, which we think will set to rest our quest for achieving more. yes, there is a need for being more mindful.

Jaggi Vasudev, a mystic, yogi, and author of the book ***Inner Engineering: A Yogi's Guide to Joy*** – commonly known as Sadhguru – has explained the rationale behind the never-ending aspirations of human beings to achieve more and more. He explains that man is consistently inventing new things to make life comfortable and more fun. Take this example: in the olden days, our ancestors used to travel by horse or bullock carts, which took longer and was not a comfortable way to commute. With the intention to make life more comfortable, man has been exploring and inventing consistently. And today we have faster vehicles; now we can fly across the countries

The Mindful Mind

in a matter of hours. And we're not stopping there. You might have heard the news that Elon Musk through his company SpaceX has shared his plans to make travel between any country in less than an hour a possibility.

But still humans are not feeling happy and fulfilled, despite all the comfort and amenities we have. Sadhguru explains that the efforts of adding one more layer of comfort in a human's life every now and then doesn't serve the key requirement; rather it merely amounts to horizontal growth. He states further that unfortunately, humans endowed with the precious gift of consciousness cannot feel everlasting happiness or fulfillment, unless there is some vertical progress. The vertical progress means that there has to be an elevation in the human consciousness. There are different ways of progressing in horizontally and vertically. While the horizontal progress is all outward and in the material world, the vertical progress can happen only in the inner world of consciousness.

Mindfulness involves being aware that your inner world is a vertical journey and

The Mindful Mind

therefore provides the real benefits from spiritual as well as material world perspective, which we will look at in greater details in the next section.

From Corporate to Government: Mindfulness Is Everywhere Now

This small section will highlight that concept of mindfulness, which was sacred and mainly originated as spiritual and religious practices in the eastern world is now gaining a strong foothold in every facet of modern life in the western world. There is definitely a scientific research and evidence highlighting the tremendous benefits arising from mindfulness, which has triggered its proliferation in every functional aspect of our lives.

Let's quickly look at some facts, which will help you convince yourself that there is something fundamental behind the mindfulness practices, which has prompted its wider acceptance across the world.

Mindfulness in Government

The Mindful Mind

The role of mindfulness in the functioning of the government becomes more important, because it involves making policies and regulations that have an impact on a larger population.

Tim Ryan, a member of U.S. House of Representatives and author of the bestselling book *"A Mindful Nation"* states that in meetings in Washington, mindfulness helps him manage his responses to peers who may say things to annoy other persons. He's even started weekly meditation meetings for congress members and staff of both parties[vii]. That makes sense because meditation helps to develop the ability of the mind to step in between stimulus and the habitual reaction.

Also, Jon Kabat-Zinn talked about his experience about a trip to UK Parliament in 2015, and stated that he was amazed to see that UK Parliament had been organizing a

---

[vii]

https://www.forbes.com/sites/alicegwalton/2014/12/14/60-minutes-explores-the-rise-of-mindfulness-meditation-and-how-it-can-change-the-brain/#d77874f768b3

The Mindful Mind

common session of mindfulness for his MPs and House of Lords Representative. He stated that Swedish Government was also implementing the mindfulness practice session[viii].

Mindfulness in Schools:

It is also reported that Tim Ryan has also worked to secure $1 million in funding to teach mindfulness to schoolchildren in his Ohio district. *"I've seen it transform classrooms, I've seen it heal veterans, I've seen what it does to individuals who have really high levels of chronic stress.... I wouldn't be willing to stick my neck out this far if I didn't think it was the thing that can help shift the country"*, as Ryan states[ix]

Mindfulness in Corporate world

[viii] https://www.mindful.org/jon-kabat-zinn-mindfulness-and-mainstream-government/

[ix] https://www.forbes.com/sites/alicegwalton/2014/12/14/60-minutes-explores-the-rise-of-mindfulness-meditation-and-how-it-can-change-the-brain/#d77874f768b3

The Mindful Mind

As you noted in the previous sections how major corporate like Google had already been conducting the mindfulness sessions to improve the performance level and mental capability of its employees. It was reported[x] that that one of the job perks at Google, is that its 52,000 employees are given free lessons in mindfulness. Google's Chade-Meng Tan, is charged with responsibilities, as his official job description is to "*Enlighten minds, open hearts, create world peace.*" Some meetings at Google start out with a couple of minutes of meditation. Not only does adding meditation to the work day make people happier and more present, but it also makes people more productive. The trick, says Tan, is to "*get into that frame of mind on demand,*" and meditation teaches people to do exactly this.

Another article[xi] describes the growth in mindfulness in the West and cites General

---

[x]
https://www.forbes.com/sites/alicegwalton/2014/12/14/60-minutes-explores-the-rise-of-mindfulness-meditation-and-how-it-can-change-the-brain/#d77874f768b3
[xi] https://www.ft.com/content/d9cb7940-ebea-11e1-

The Mindful Mind

Mills as one company that is making it an integral part of its company culture.

> "[General Mills] has even begun research into its efficacy, and the early results are striking. After one of Marturano's seven-week courses, 83 percent of participants said they were "taking time each day to optimize my personal productivity" – up from 23 percent before the course. Eighty-two percent said they now make time to eliminate tasks with limited productivity value – up from 32 percent before the course. And among senior executives who took the course, 80 percent reported a positive change in their ability to make better decisions, while 89 percent said they became better listeners".

One another report[xii] stated that organizations such as Aetna, Mayo Clinic,

---

985a-00144feab49a#axzz2ApW2UUXh

[xii] http://journals.sagepub.com/doi/10.1177/0149206315617003

The Mindful Mind

and the U.S. Army use mindfulness training to improve workplace functioning.

Mindfulness in Prisons:

Mindfulness has been taught in prisons, to reduce hostility and mood disturbance among inmates, and to improve their self-esteem. Additional studies indicate that mindfulness interventions can result in significant reductions in anger, substance abuse, increased relaxation capacity, self-regulation, and optimism[xiii].

The world is realizing the importance of Mindfulness. Vietnamese Buddhist monk Thích Nhất Hạnh in his book *'Peace is Every Step'* has rightly stated:

> *"Life can be found only in the present moment. The past is gone, the future is not yet here, and if we do not go back to ourselves in the present moment,*

[xiii] https://en.wikipedia.org/wiki/Mindfulness

The Mindful Mind

we cannot be in touch with life."

The Mindful Mind

PART III: The Magic of Mindfulness-Mega Benefits

****

Healing and uplifting our brain, mind and heart is now an imperative for us collectively so we can deal with the tsunami of very real technological advances rushing towards us, changing life as we know it forever. – Jonathan Robert Banks

This section of the book will help those people who are still a bit skeptical to adopt

The Mindful Mind

mindfulness as a part of their daily routines. Let's admit that to some people sitting silently in any posture doing nothing might be a dull and even tedious task. Moreover, you should not adopt mindfulness practice for the sake of just doing it, or because everyone talks about it. As Jon Kabat-Zinn recommends you must probe your deepest 'why' before you start it.

At the same time, I think you would be curious to check out why big corporate giants like Google, Apple, Facebook etc. are deploying mindfulness sessions in their organization. You would also be inquisitive to understand why the top performance and billionaires of the likes of Steve Jobs; Arnold Schwarzenegger have chosen to start their days with a form of meditation. You already have a hunch there are definitely some bigger reasons, or why would successful companies or people spend their mornings practicing it?

The purpose of this section is to highlight the magical effects, supported by scientific evidence that mindfulness has on our brain and bodies. You will notice how mindfulness

The Mindful Mind

can physically change the structure of your brain and how it can improve your health.

So let's get started.

It Changes the Structure Of Your Brain

Some people might not know that, until quite recently most brain research had been done on animals. The introduction of Magnetic Resonance Imagining (MRI) into clinical practice in last few decades has resulted in substantial scientific advancement. It has enabled researchers to measure the activity and changes in the individual parts of the brain in humans.

Sara Lazar, a neuroscientist at Harvard Medical School, used the MRI technology to look at very fine, and detailed brain structures to observe the inner physical changes in the brain while a person is performing a certain task, including yoga and meditation.

Lazar tells her own story of her initial experiences with yoga. She states she used to be skeptical about the tall claims made by

The Mindful Mind

her yoga teacher about the emotional benefits of meditations to human beings. It was only after attending several classes, when she indeed felt calmer, happier, and more compassionate, then she decided to re-focus her research on the changes in the brain's physical structure as a result of meditation practice.

In her first study[xiv], Lazar looked at individuals with extensive meditation experience, which involved focused attention on internal experiences (no mantras or chanting). The data proved, among others, that meditation may slow down or prevent age-related thinning of the frontal cortex that otherwise contributes to the formation of memories. The common knowledge says that when people get older, they tend to forget stuff. Interestingly, Lazar and her team found out that 40–50-year-old meditators had the same amount of gray matter in their cortex as the 20–30-year-old ones.

[xiv]

https://www.ncbi.nlm.nih.gov/pmc/articles/PMC1361002/

The Mindful Mind

For her second study[xv], she engaged people who had never meditated before and put them through a Mindfulness-Based Stress Reduction training program, where they took a weekly class and were told to perform mindfulness exercises, including body scan, mindful yoga, and sitting meditation, every day for 30 to 40 minutes. Lazar wanted to test the participants for positive effects of mindfulness meditation on their psychological well-being and alleviating symptoms of various disorders such as anxiety, depression, eating disorder, insomnia, or chronic pain.

After eight weeks, she found out that the brain volume increased in many regions as below

i. Hippocampus: a seahorse-shaped structure responsible for learning, storage of memories, spatial orientation, and regulation of emotions.

[xv]

https://www.ncbi.nlm.nih.gov/pmc/articles/PMC3004979/

ii. <u>Temporoparietal Junction</u>: the area where temporal and parietal lobes meet and which is responsible for empathy and compassion.

On the other hand, the one area whose brain volume decreased was:

<u>Amygdala</u>: an almond-shaped structure responsible for triggering the fight-or-flight response as a reaction to a threat, whether real or only perceived.

Therefore, you can observe that people practicing meditation can have remarkable and positive changes in the key regions of their mind, to help them perform better and lead a happier life.

Meta-analysis of multiple Brain Studies- Numerous Benefits

Over last more than a decade, researchers have carried out numerous neuroimaging studies to investigate how the brain's gray and white matter may be shaped by meditation. One meta-analysis[xvi] of 2014, for

---

[xvi] https://www.ncbi.nlm.nih.gov/pubmed/24705269

The Mindful Mind

the purpose of consolidating the results, pooled data from 21 neuroimaging studies wherein the brains of about 300 experienced meditation practitioners were examined. The analysis concluded that certain brain regions were consistently altered in the experienced meditators as stated below:

- <u>Rostrolateral prefrontal cortex</u>: A region associated with meta-awareness (awareness of how you think), introspection, and processing of complex, abstract information.

- <u>Sensory cortices and insular cortex</u>: The main cortical hubs for processing of tactile information such touch, pain, conscious proprioception, and body awareness.

- <u>Hippocampus</u>: A pair of subcortical structures involved in memory formation and facilitating emotional responses.

- <u>Anterior cingulate cortex and mid-cingulate cortex</u>: Cortical regions involved in self-regulation, emotional regulation, attention, and self-control.

- <u>Superior longitudinal fasciculus and corpus callosum</u>: Subcortical white matter tracts that communicate within and between brain hemispheres.

Mindfulness –the Default Mode Versus Direct Experience

> *"Being mindful is not a matter of thinking more clearly about experience; it is the act of experiencing more clearly"* — *Sam Harris*

There was another study conducted in 2007 called *Mindfulness meditation reveals distinct neural modes of self-reference*[xvii],

---

[xvii] https://academic.oup.com/scan/article/2/4/313/1676557

The Mindful Mind

wherein Norman Farb at the University of Toronto, along with few other scientists, revealed an intriguing viewpoint to understand mindfulness from a neuroscience perspective.

Farb and his colleagues conducted the research to examine how humans experience their own moment-to-moment experience. They discovered that people have two distinct ways of interacting with the world, using two different sets of networks. One network involves what is called the *'default mode network'*, which includes regions of the medial prefrontal cortex, along with memory regions such as the hippocampus. This network is called default because it becomes active when not much else is happening, and you think about yourself.

If you are at a hill station and sitting amid a serene and natural beauty of hills valley around, then you would have realized that sometimes instead of enjoying those moments, you find yourself engrossed in the thoughts of what you'll see next. You will be thinking about how your office is going on,

The Mindful Mind

or how your subordinates or colleagues are handling that nasty email received from your client. All this thinking is called your default network in operation, whose role is always planning or ruminating.

This default network also become active when you think about yourself or other people, it holds together a *'narrative'*. A narrative is a story line with characters interacting with each other over time. The brain holds vast stores of information about your own and other people's history. When the default network is active, you are thinking about your history and future and all the people you know, including yourself, and how this enormous tapestry of information weaves together – and in Farb's study, they call it as narrative circuitry.

When you experience the world using this narrative network, you take in information from the outside world, process it through a filter of what everything means, and add your own interpretations. With this narrative circuit in action, even if you are standing on a serene natural hilly area, you are making up your own stories about the

The Mindful Mind

current scenario, rather than being in a real-time presence. Therefore, you can conclude that the default network is quite automatic and is active for most of your waking moments without any efforts on your side.

The Farb study shows there is a whole other way of feeling the experience. Scientists call this type of experience as *direct experience.* When the *'direct experience network'* is active, several different brain regions become more active. This includes the insula, a region that relates to perceiving bodily sensations. The anterior cingulate cortex is also activated, which is a region central to switching your attention.

Here comes the best part. When this direct experience network is activated, you are not thinking intently about the past or future, or anything else. Rather, you are experiencing information coming into your senses in real time. While sitting on a rock on a hilly area, your whole attention is on the nature around you. You are filled with curiosity, awe, and so enthralled by the natural allure, which is experienced through another perspective of *direct experience.*

The Mindful Mind

How *'default mode'* and *'direct experience'* can be used efficiently?

You can experience the world through your narrative circuitry, which will be useful for planning, goal setting, and strategizing. Also, you can experience the world more directly, which enables you to perceive more sensory information. Experiencing the world through the direct experience network allows you to get closer to the reality of any event. You perceive more as well as accurate information about events occurring around you. Noticing more real-time information makes you more flexible in how you respond to the world. You also become less imprisoned by the past, your habits, expectations or assumptions, and more able to respond to events as they unfold.

In the Farb's experiment, people who regularly practiced noticing the *narrative* and *direct experience* paths, such as regular meditators, had realization about the stronger differentiation between the two paths. By this awareness, they always knew which path they were on at any time, and could switch between them more easily. On

The Mindful Mind

the other hand, people who had not practiced noticing these paths were more likely to automatically take the narrative path i.e. guided only by their past pattern and behavior or engaged in future thinking and missing the real time information.

Above is thoroughly backed by another study[xviii] by Kirk Brown, where he found that people high on a mindfulness scale were more aware of their unconscious processes. Additionally these people had more cognitive control, and a greater ability to shape what they do and what they say, than people lower on the mindfulness scale. Also, a clinical intervention study with cancer patients demonstrates that increases in mindfulness over time relate to declines in mood disturbance and stress.

If you're in the midst of scenic beauty surrounded by nature and if you're someone with a good level or mindfulness, you are more likely to realize that you are ruining the experience of this beauty by

---

[xviii] http://www.refdoc.fr/Detailnotice?cpsidt=15556264

The Mindful Mind

unnecessarily worrying about some future event, and therefore focus on to the snow-clad mountains. When you make this change in your attention, you change the functioning of your brain, and this can have a long-term impact on how your brain works too.

Mindfulness to cure your bad habits:

Bad Habits are nothing but addictions. If you smoke, drink, or watch TV late at night, despite knowing that you have to rush to the office next day early morning, then this is nothing but an addiction.

Judson Brewer, director of the Therapeutic Neuroscience Laboratory at the Center for Mindfulness in Medicine, Health Care, and Society at the University of Massachusetts Medical School and author of *The Craving Mind: From Cigarettes to Smartphones to Love – Why We Get Hooked and How We Can Break Bad Habits* advocates the use of mindfulness for breaking any bad habit. Yes, he claims that mindfulness can be said as

The Mindful Mind

'gold standard' for treating cigarette addiction patients.

In the first place, we need to ask this very question: why do we have bad habits in the first place?

It is because when you are going through stress, anxiety, or not feeling good in any manner, then you try to find something which makes you feel good. So you do something that has made you feel good in the past.. You had the experience of numbing your brain for sometime through the use of nicotine or alcohol for a short time. That short term pleasure now takes the form of an addiction.

Brewer suggests that mindfulness is the tool through which you can get rid of your addiction and he terms this 4 step mindfulness formula to cure bad habit as "RAIN: Recognize, Accept, Investigate, and Note.

Brewer explains that in order to get rid of any bad habits or so called addiction, there are four stages involved and directly or

The Mindful Mind

indirectly it involves mindfulness of the situation carefully. Let's elaborate this one by one by taking example of any of your addictions.

1. <u>Recognize:</u> Whenever you feel a craving for smoke or drink, or say eating another cup-cake, the first step is to recognize the feeling of craving in your body. In my case, while writing this book, I am intermittently thinking of switching my attention to something different which will give me instant gratification, like checking something on Facebook. Once you realize what you're craving, you shouldn't immediately run to grab that thing or get trapped by that emotional feeling, rather you need to *'recognize'* that feeling at that moment.

2. <u>Accept:</u> The next step is to 'accept' that feeling arising in your body. That's bit tricky and difficult. It often hurts. Now the good part is you don't have to do anything yet. But the

The Mindful Mind

difficult stuff is that you are feeling uncomfortable and want to scratch that itch, but you can't do that. Brewer recommended that you have to acknowledge your acceptance in a small active way, like nod your head or just say, '*okay, I got you*'.

3. <u>Investigate:</u> The next logical step in the process is the thinking work. You have to analyse the reason behind your bad habit or addiction. Why do you want to go out and get a smoke? Why do I want to switch the tab and get distracted while writing? You shouldn't compel your mind not to think about that, rather you have to arouse curiosity about why that craving is coming. Here is the role of mindfulness. As your craving grows, you see how it feels in your body. The main point here is to get disengaged with that thought of craving. Precisely for the reason that you are not that thought. You are separate from that thought.

The Mindful Mind

4. <u>Note:</u> The fourth step is to take mental note of the emotions arising in your body. Just give a single word or short phrase to put a label on what you feel. There is a neuroscience behind this noting. Taking a note of emotion reduces the impact of the emotions. Alex Korb, PhD in his book *The Upward Spiral* explains the science behind this mental noting as below:

"...in one fMRI study, appropriately titled "Putting Feelings into Words" participants viewed pictures of people with emotional facial expressions. Predictably, each participant's amygdala activated to the emotions in the picture. But when they were asked to name the emotion, the ventrolateral prefrontal cortex activated and reduced the emotional amygdala reactivity. In other words, consciously recognizing the emotions reduced their impact."

The Mindful Mind

Mindful Munching to Lose Your Weight:

Lilian Cheugn, a lecturer at Harvard School of Public Health and co-author (with Buddhist monk Thich Nhat Hanh) of the book titled, *Savor: Mindful Eating, Mindful Life*, professes about applying ancient mindfulness techniques to eating in the modern world. "It is not just what we consume, but how we cat, whcn we eat, why we eat, and whom we eat with that makes a difference," says Cheung in an article reported in Harvard Magazine[xix]. She continues "We nutritionists can talk all we want about the best diets, but until people understand the physical, psychological, cultural, and environmental factors that make us binge, they will almost always continue to overeat."

"When we eat and our mind is aware of each bite, savoring the taste and the nourishment it gives us, we are already practicing mindfulness," Cheung and Hanh write in the book. This definition differs slightly from

---

[xix] https://harvardmagazine.com/2010/09/mindful-munching

The Mindful Mind

Ellen Langer's non-meditational version, but the two share a central premise: people who pay attention to new things in the present can effect change at any time.

Often, we become trapped in cycles of guilt, Cheung explains, anxious about what we ate, what we failed to do. "Each minute we spend worrying about the future and regretting the past is a minute we miss in our appointment with life," the authors write.

By applying the four noble truths of Buddhism to our eating habits—(1) that we have suffering in our lives (our excess weight); (2) that we can identify the causes of our suffering (too many sugar-sweetened beverages, mindless television watching, emotional eating); (3) that healing is possible (negative habits can be changed); and (4) that there are paths to free us from our pain (mindfulness)—people can better navigate the factors that affect their weight as the book explains.

What we eat is as important as our relationship with food, Cheung explains. As she and Hanh write in their book, *"It is the*

The Mindful Mind

awareness of the present moment, the realization of why we do what we do, that enables us to stop feeling bad and start changing our behavior.

The Benefits of Mindfulness- Summarized

As you noted that the scientific studies have clearly shown the physical changes in our brain structure which shows qualitative improvement in the functions of the body. If someone consistently practices meditation, then the concept of neuroplasticity comes into play. Neuroplasticity is the ability of your brain reorganizing itself, both physically and functionally, throughout your life due to your environment, behavior, thinking, and emotions. It means you can start thinking differently by making changes in your environment and your thinking patterns. The science has concluded that there is no such thing such as a fixed or only-once wired mind. Rather, it has the potential to keep changing during one's lifetime. In my other book *The Mindset Makeover*, I have explained in detail how neuroplasticity works to change your brain.

The Mindful Mind

Now let's summarize the key benefits of mindfulness as below:

a. **Improves Focus**: As backed by science, mindfulness improves the gray matter in the hippocampus area of your brain, which is responsible amongst other items for learning more and better memory.

b. **Reduce Stress and Anxiety**: The amygdala portion of the brain is responsible for fight, flight or freeze responses. It is the fear center of our brain. The scientific studies have already evidenced that the mindfulness has the impact of reducing the size of amygdala in our brain. It also reduces the level of cortisol (the stress hormones) in our brain and thus to control.

c. **Improve Emotional Intelligence**: Consistently watching your thoughts and emotions curtails your tendency to be reactive upon the arousal of emotions like anger or stress. Since

The Mindful Mind

you are the person who is witnessing the emotions and therefore can rationally decide looking for distance about whether a particular emotion is going to help you or will make you repent later. Mindfulness practice helps you to develop emotional intelligence.

d. **Improves Clarity**: Through the mindfulness practice over a period of time, you can start watching your thoughts, emotions and feeling as different from yourself. The key benefit is that you realize that you are not your thought and thus develop the habit of not getting swayed with every other thoughts and emotion. It leads to getting clarity about your life and the direction you need to consistently go.

e. **Improves Intuition**: Intuition is the ability of our body to listen to the signals popping up in our minds every moment. But often due to our rational mind and due to our habits of over

The Mindful Mind

thinking, we tend to ignore this inner voice. The key reason for suppressing this voice of intuition is our fearful thinking about probable adverse outcomes. With mindfulness practice, you develop your capacity to observe all your thoughts and emotions. Therefore, while on the one hand, it helps to build your immunity to get affected from the negative or fearful thinking, on the other hand, it develops your ability to pay closer attention to the subtle tone of your intuition for taking any action.

f. **Improves Compassion And Empathy**. As scientific studies show that mindfulness practice improve the grey material in the temporoparietal junction of the brain, which is responsible for empathy and compassion.

g. **Develops calmness**: Mindfulness practices requires you to focus on breath and other movements in your body. The natural consequence of

The Mindful Mind

observing the bodily function in itself makes them slower. If you consistently watch your brain, you will realized after 5-10 breathes that your body starts relaxing. With the relax body, your mind becomes calm and peaceful. This state of mind helps you to think clearly and you start attracting the solutions to your problems.

h. **Slows Down The Ageing Of Brain**: Mindfulness practices have shown to improve the gray matter in the prefrontal cortex of our brain, which area is responsible for working memory and executive decision making. The studies conducted by Sara Lazer showed that the brains of fifty-year-old people who meditate were shown to have amount of gray material equivalent to someone aged twenty-five.

You would agree that developing mindfulness practice in our day-to-day life

The Mindful Mind

considering the huge benefits it entails, is a no-brainer. Also, the fact that the benefits to our body and brain function are so adequately established by scientific evidence, that there is no reason to not experiment this in our routine.

With that, we will now move to next section, which will explain you the ways to start the mindfulness practice.

******

The Mindful Mind

PART IV: Mindfulness – Let's Do It

****

Too often, our lives cease working because we cease working at life, because we are unwilling to take responsibility for things as they are, and to work with our difficulties." ~ Jon Kabat-Zinn

In the previous sections, you had learned about the background of the mindfulness from eastern and western perspectives. You also explored the scientific studies evidencing the benefits of meditation. Now, after knowing the multiple advantages of

The Mindful Mind

mindfulness, the next logical step should be to explore the best ways to implement mindfulness practice into your life. This section of the book is specifically exploring a few mindfulness techniques and how to start doing it to get the best possible benefits out of it.

Also, to clarify that the key objective of the book is strengthening your mental faculties and cognitive abilities, to help you perform better and live an enriched life and not from any spiritual or religious perspective. The beneficial effects from a spiritual perspective are the natural outcome and you will start realizing once you regularly follow the mindfulness practice.

Therefore, I have captured a few mindfulness techniques, which are easy to implement in your everyday life without taking much of your time. You will also find the reference of some valuable resources from top mindfulness experts, if you have some interest to pursue your journey further.

So let's get directly into it.

The Mindful Mind

How Should You Sit?

Mindfulness is all about being stable in your mind and body, so you can watch your thoughts and emotions floating in your entire body. So the first step towards that is to make your body stable by sitting in a calm position.

Jon Kabat-Zinn in his book, *Wherever You Go There You Are,* elaborates on how to sit for your mindfulness practice. In his words:

> "When we describe the sitting posture, the word that feels the most appropriate is "dignity."
>
> Sitting down to meditate, our posture talks to us. It makes its own statement. You might say the posture itself is the meditation. If we slump, it reflects low energy, passivity, a lack of clarity. If we sit ramrod-straight, we are tense, making too much of an effort, trying too hard. When I use the word "dignity" in teaching situations, as in "Sit in a way that embodies dignity," everybody immediately adjusts their posture to sit up

The Mindful Mind

straighter. But they don't stiffen. Faces relax, shoulders drop, head, neck, and back come into easy alignment. The spine rises out of the pelvis with energy. Sometimes people tend to sit forward, away from the backs of their chairs, more autonomously. Everybody seems to instantly know that inner feeling of dignity and how to embody it."

The central idea is whether you are sitting in a chair or in a more formal meditation posture, keep the word *dignity* in mind.

Develop Your One-pointedness Muscle

The key foundation of mindfulness practice is concentration. The more your mind is stable and calm, the more robust your mindfulness practice will be. Again Jon Kabat-Zinn beautifully explains in his book:

"You can think of concentration as the capacity of the mind to sustain an unwavering attention on one object of observation. It is cultivated by attending to one thing, such as the breath, and just

The Mindful Mind

limiting one's focus to that. In Sanskrit, concentration is called samadhi, or "one-pointedness." Samadhi is developed and deepened by continually bringing the attention back to the breath every time it wanders. When practicing strictly concentrative forms of meditation, we purposefully refrain from any efforts to inquire into areas such as where the mind went when it wandered off, or that the quality of the breath fluctuates. Our energy is directed solely towards experiencing this breath coming in, this breath going out, or some other single object of attention. With extended practice, the mind tends to become better and better at staying on the breath, or noticing even the earliest impulse to become distracted by something else, and either resisting its pull in the first place and staying on the breath, or quickly returning to it."

How to do it?

Mindfulness meditation expert Sam Harris compares doing meditation like walking on a rope easy to explain but difficult to master, but then goes on to describe the steps need to do your mindfulness practice as below[xx].

The Mindful Mind

"The practice of mindfulness is extraordinarily simple to describe, but it is in no sense easy. True mastery probably requires special talent and a lifetime of practice. Thus, the simple instructions given below are analogous to instructions on how to walk a tightrope—which, I assume, go something like this:

1. Find a horizontal cable that can support your weight.

2. Stand on one end.

3. Step forward by placing one foot directly in front of the other.

4. Repeat.

5. Don't fall.

Clearly, steps 3-5 entail a little practice. Happily, the benefits of training in meditation arrive long before mastery ever does. And falling, from the point of view of vipassana (another breathe focused meditation technique), occurs

---

[xx] https://www.samharris.org/blog/item/how-to-meditate

The Mindful Mind

ceaselessly, every moment that one becomes lost in thought. The problem is not thoughts themselves but the state of thinking without knowing that one is thinking.

As every meditator soon discovers, such distraction is the normal condition of our minds: Most of us fall from the wire every second, toppling headlong—whether gliding happily in reverie, or plunging into fear, anger, self-hatred and other negative states of mind. Meditation is a technique for breaking this spell, if only for a few moments. The goal is to awaken from our trance of discursive thinking—and from the habit of ceaselessly grasping at the pleasant and recoiling from the unpleasant—so that we can enjoy a mind that is undisturbed by worry, merely open like the sky, and effortlessly aware of the flow of experience in the present.

> *"So plastic is mind, so receptive, that the slightest thought*

The Mindful Mind

makes an impression upon it. People who think many kinds of thought must expect to receive a confused manifestation in their lives. If a gardener plants a thousand kinds of seeds, he will get a thousand kinds of plants: it is the same in mind." — Dr. Ernest Holmes

Meditation Instructions:

1. Sit comfortably, with your spine erect, either in a chair or cross-legged on a cushion.

2. Close your eyes, take a few deep breaths, and feel the points of contact between your body and the chair or floor. Notice the sensations associated with sitting—feelings of pressure, warmth, tingling, vibration, etc.

The Mindful Mind

3. Gradually become aware of the process of breathing. Pay attention to wherever you feel your breath most clearly—either at the nostrils, or in the rising and falling your abdomen.

4. Allow your attention to rest in the mere sensation of breathing. (There is no need to control your breath. Just let it come and go naturally.)

5. Every time your mind wanders, gently return it to the sensation of breathing.

6. As you focus on your breath, you will notice that other perceptions and sensations continue to appear: sounds, feelings in the body, emotions, etc. Simply notice these phenomena as they emerge in the field of awareness, and then return to the sensation of breathing.

The Mindful Mind

7. The moment you observe that you have been lost in thought, notice the present thought itself as an object of consciousness. Then return your attention to the breath—or to whatever sounds or sensations arise in the next moment.

8. Continue in this way until you can merely witness all objects of consciousness—sights, sounds, sensations, emotions, and even thoughts themselves—as they arise and pass away.

9. Don't fall.

Those who are new to the practice generally find it useful to hear instructions of this kind spoken aloud, in the form of a guided meditation."

There are plenty of guided meditation apps available these days, which can help you to do a guided meditation, few of those are detailed later in this section.

The Mindful Mind

In addition to formal seated practice, we can also bring in the practice of mindfulness during our daily activities: while eating, walking, and talking. For meditation practice in daily life, the practice is to pay attention to what is going on in the present moment, to be aware of what is happening – and not live unconsciously. If you are eating, that means paying attention to the food you are eating, its smell, how you chew it, and how you swallow food. If you are walking, that means being more aware of your body movements, your feet touching the ground, the sounds you are hearing, etc.

Your effort in seated practice meditation supports your daily life practice, and vice-versa. They are both equally important.

Stress & Depression: If You Can't Cope Up Alone
Overcome Stress and Depression with Mindfulness Therapies

As you are noticing that mindfulness, if implemented in our daily lives, can really do wonders in almost any area of our life. But, every human being has different background

The Mindful Mind

and life circumstances. More often people find it difficult to cope up with the day to day stress and anxiety and they tend to get into depression. In such case, people sometime lose willpower and determination to work on putting their life back on track. Also staying longer in such situation is not advisable as it only worsens the situation. Therefore, in such cases, there arises a need of some outside help to handle the situation better.

Realizing this Jon Kabat-Zinn, invented Mindfulness based programs in 1979 and created the Stress Reduction Clinic and the Center for Mindfulness in Medicine, Health Care, and Society at the University of Massachusetts Medical School. This program is known as Mindfulness based Stress Reduction (MBSR) programs and conducted widely across the world.

Kabat-Zinn studied the practices of mindfulness and meditations from Buddhist teachers such as Thich Nhat Hanh and Zen Master Seung Sahn. His practice of yoga and studies with Buddhist teachers led him to integrate their teachings with scientific findings. MBSR uses yoga,

The Mindful Mind

body awareness, and mindfulness meditation to help people become more mindful.

MBSR program is an 8-week program conducted physically as well as online too. If someone wishes to expedite the process, they can opt for a 5 day residential program at different location organized by Center for Mindfulness.

MBSR is a structured group program that employs mindfulness meditation to alleviate suffering associated with physical, psychosomatic and psychiatric disorders. The program, nonreligious and nonesoteric, is based upon a systematic procedure to develop enhanced awareness of moment-to-moment experience of perceptible mental processes.[xxi]

Research has shown that mindfulness based stress reduction has helped people with chronic diseases. Participation in an MBSR program is likely to result in coping better with symptoms, improved overall well-being

---

[xxi] https://www.ncbi.nlm.nih.gov/pubmed/15256293

The Mindful Mind

and quality of life, and enhanced health outcomes.[xxii]

There is another set Mindfulness based program known as Mindfulness based Cognitive Therapy. As per the website of Center for Mindfulness[xxiii], Mindfulness-Based Cognitive Therapy (MBCT) is an established program to help people who are prone to recurrent depression. MBCT combines the practice and clinical application of mindfulness meditation with the tools of cognitive therapy to break the cycle of recurrent depression, and is based on the research of Drs. Zindel Segal, John Teasdale and Mark Williams, and documented in their book *Mindfulness-Based Cognitive Therapy for Depression, a New Approach to Preventing Relapse.*

The Center for Mindfulness also conducts the MBCT program realizing people who are suffering from depressions would get benefitted from this. Since this is based on

---

[xxii]

https://www.ncbi.nlm.nih.gov/pubmed/20815988
[xxiii] https://www.umassmed.edu/cfm/mindfulness-based-programs/mbct-courses/about-mbct/

The Mindful Mind

mindfulness only, it expands the mission of the CFM to offer an evidence-based program designed specifically for people who struggle with depression. As per CFM, it offers participants an opportunity to learn a new way of relating to unwanted thoughts and feelings and powerful skills for responding to them in an intentional and skilful manner. Participants report feeling a sense of freedom from the trap of emotional suffering that may have been present for many years. While people with a history of depression can benefit from MBSR, MBCT is specifically designed to reveal how depression operates and provide specific tools for this condition. For more details, you can visit the website of Center for Mindfulness at https://www.umassmed.edu/cfm

Mindfulness made Mobile - On the Go

For some people sitting on their own and watching their breathing can be a difficult task. They might need some initial guidance to start with. Thankfully there are plenty of mobile apps out there, which provided guided meditation through instructions.

The Mindful Mind

Starting with these apps helps you to get into a sitting habit for dedicated time and experience the inner world.

Here are some of the best apps, you can start using to develop mindfulness meditation practice.

- **Headspace:** They call it "A gym membership for the mind," Headspace provides a series of guided meditation sessions and mindfulness training.
- **Stop Breath and Think:** This app will help you to check in with how you're feeling and try short activities tuned to your emotions.
- **Calm:** The name speaks of itself very well. The moment you open this app, you might feel a sense of calm and peace. Relaxing sounds of falling rain play automatically in the background. You can get a lot of free meditations over there.

The Mindful Mind

- **Welzen**- You can relax with a new 10-minute meditation plus an inspiring life lesson every day.
- **Pacifica:** -It provides guided deep breathing and muscle relaxation exercises, daily anti-anxiety experiments, and tools including a mood tracker. Recording your own thoughts can help you understand your thinking patterns and recognize possible anxiety triggers.
- **Insight Timer** is one of the most popular free meditation apps out there, and it's easy to see why. The app features more than 4,000 guided meditations from over 1,000 teachers—on topics like self-compassion, nature, and stress—plus talks and podcasts.
- **Aura** is a meditation app with a simple premise: Every day, you get a new, personalized, three-minute meditation. The same meditation never repeats; according to cofounder Daniel Lee, Aura's teachers are constantly recording new tracks. To personalize the experience, Aura

The Mindful Mind

initially asks about your age and how stressed, optimistic, and interested in mindfulness you are.

- **Omvana** is a beautiful meditation app created by personal growth company Mindvalley. Its library contains thousands of meditations, and about 75 of those are free.

I hope this section has provided you sufficient information to start with your mindfulness practice. You can follow the process on your own or can take the help of online tools to start your journey.

****

Final Words

****

"Mindfulness lets us see things in a new light and believe in the possibility of change."~ Ellen Langer

Congratulations, you have just finished reading this short and focused book. I hope you find yourself now equipped with a better understanding about the concept of mindfulness, even if you have resisted any meditation practice in the past.

You now know that mindfulness is not something, which requires you to follow certain religion or join some cult. Rather it is simply an approach to living a life, in which you are mindful and aware of everything. We

The Mindful Mind

all want to be more aware and educated about the outside world and continuously strive towards that, but often forget that if we don't pay attention to our inner world of thoughts and feelings and let them scatter around, it will not lead us to a fulfilled life in the outside world.

I also hope that this book will help you change your beliefs and shatter any myths, if you had about mindfulness. Since you have already spent your time reading this, it shows that you had all good intention to know about the subject and get the requisite benefits out of it. The next step is to spare some time daily from your routine to focus on our inner world and start reaping the benefits of it.

I wish you a life of inner calm and outer riches, and that's real and holistic success.

Cheers,

Som Bathla

The Mindful Mind

Thank You!

Before you go, I would like to say thank you for purchasing and reading my book.

You could have picked amongst dozens of other books on this subject, but you took a chance and checked out this one.

So, big thanks for downloading this book and reading all the way to the end.

Now I'd like to ask for a small favor. **Could you please spend a minute or two and leave a review for this book on your Online Book Store?**

Reviews are really gold for authors!

Your reviews will help me continue to write the kind of books that help you get results. Also, your review will help the book to reach out to more readers.

So, just drop in 1-2 lines of your honest review on the book.

The Mindful Mind

Your Free Gift Bundle:

Did you download your Gift Bundle already?

Click and Download your Free Gift Bundle Below

Claim Your Gift Bundle!

Three AMAZING BOOKS for FREE on:

1. Mind Hacking - in just 21 days!
2. Time Hacking- How to Cheat Time!
3. The Productivity Manifesto

Download Now

You can also download your gift at http://sombathla.com/freegiftbundle

About the Author

Som Bathla writes books that focus on changing old mindsets, overcoming self-defeating behavior & best strategies for enhancing the productivity and resourcefulness in all areas of life.

He has written more than half a dozen books on above subject and his many books have already touched the Amazon #1 Best Seller. He has good plans to continuously create more action guides to help readers to lead a productive and resourceful life (for details visit sombathla.com)

He is convinced about the limitlessness of the human potential and strongly believes that everyone has the potential of achieving more than one thinks about oneself. His life mantra is that a rewarding life is nothing but

The Mindful Mind

a series of small actions taken consistently on a daily basis with a positive and resourceful mindset.

Som resides in India where he spends most of his time reading, writing and enjoying time with his amazing wife and two sweet daughters. He is deeply committed to a path of never-ending self-improvement and open to explore the best possibilities coming on his journey.

More Books by Som Bathla

WHAT IF I FAIL?: Leverage your Fear of Failure & Turn into Fuel for Success, Rewire your Belief System, Learn to Trigger Action despite being Scared and Take Charge of Your Life

THE MINDSET MAKEOVER: Transform Your Mindset to Attract Success, Unleash Your True Potential, Control Thoughts and Emotions, Become Unstoppable and Achieve Your Goals Faster

The Mindful Mind

<u>Living Beyond Self Doubt: Reprogram Your Insecure Mindset, Reduce Stress and Anxiety, Boost Your Confidence, Take Massive Action despite Being Scared & Reclaim Your Dream Life</u>

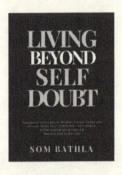

<u>FOCUS MASTERY: Master Your Attention, Ignore Distractions, Make Better Decisions Faster and Accelerate Your Success</u>

The Mindful Mind

JUST GET IT DONE: Conquer Procrastination, Eliminate Distractions, Boost Your Focus, Take Massive Action Proactively and Get Difficult Things Done Faster

Master Your Day- Design Your Life: Develop Growth Mindset, Build Routines to Level-Up your Day, Deal Smartly with Outside World and Craft Your Dream Life

The Mindful Mind

<u>The 30 Hour Day: Develop Achiever's Mindset and Habits, Work Smarter and Still Create Time For Things That Matter</u>

<u>The Quoted Life: 223 Best Inspirational and Motivational Quotes on Success, Mindset, Confidence, Learning, Persistence, Motivation, and Happiness</u>

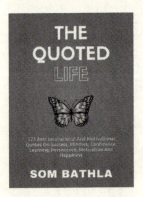

The Mindful Mind

Copyright © 2017 by Som Bathla

All rights reserved. No part of this book may be reproduced in any form without permission in writing from the author.

No part of this publication may be reproduced or transmitted in any form or by any means, mechanical or electronic, including photocopying or recording, or by any information storage and retrieval system, or transmitted by email or by any other means whatsoever without permission in writing from the author.

DISCLAIMER

While all attempts have been made to verify the information provided in this publication, the author does not assume any responsibility for errors, omissions, or contrary interpretations of the subject matter herein.

The views expressed are those of the author alone, and should not be taken as expert instruction or commands. The reader is responsible for his or her own actions.

The author makes no representations or warranties with respect to the accuracy or completeness of the contents of this work

The Mindful Mind

and specifically disclaims all warranties, including without limitation warranties of fitness for a particular purpose. No warranty may be created or extended by sales or promotional materials. The advice and recipes contained herein may not be suitable for everyone. This work is sold with the understanding that the author is not engaged in rendering medical, legal or other professional advice or services. If professional assistance is required, the services of a competent professional person should be sought. The author shall not be liable for damages arising here from. The fact that an individual, organization of website is referred to in this work as a citation and/or potential source of further information does not mean that the author endorses the information the individual, organization to website may provide or recommendations they/it may make. Further, readers should be aware that Internet websites listed in this work might have changed or disappeared between when this work was written and when it is read.

Adherence to all applicable laws and regulations, including international, federal, state, and local governing professional licensing, business practices, advertising, and all other aspects of doing business in

The Mindful Mind

any jurisdiction in the world is the sole responsibility of the purchaser or reader.

Made in the USA
San Bernardino, CA
22 August 2018